Orange Animals

by Teddy Borth

abdopublishing.com

Published by Abdo Kids, a division of ABDO, PO Box 398166, Minneapolis, Minnesota 55439.

Copyright © 2015 by Abdo Consulting Group, Inc. International copyrights reserved in all countries. No part of this book may be reproduced in any form without written permission from the publisher.

Printed in the United States of America, North Mankato, Minnesota.

102014

012015

 THIS BOOK CONTAINS RECYCLED MATERIALS

Photo Credits: iStock, Science Source, Shutterstock

Production Contributors: Teddy Borth, Jennie Forsberg, Grace Hansen

Design Contributors: Laura Rask, Dorothy Toth

Library of Congress Control Number: 2014943662

Cataloging-in-Publication Data

Borth, Teddy.

 Orange animals / Teddy Borth.

   p. cm. -- (Animal colors)

ISBN 978-1-62970-696-2 (lib. bdg.)

Includes index.

1. Animals--Juvenile literature.   I. Title.

590--dc23

                   2014943662

Table of Contents

Orange 4

Orange on Land 6

Orange in Air 12

Orange in Water 18

More Facts 22

Glossary 23

Index 24

Abdo Kids Code 24

Orange

Orange is a **secondary color**.
Painters make orange by
mixing red and yellow.

4

Mixing Colors

⬤ + ⬤ = ⬤

⬤ + ⬤ = ⬤

⬤ + ⬤ = ⬤

⬤ + ⬤ + ⬤ = ⬤

Primary Colors

- ⬤ Red
- ⬤ Yellow
- ⬤ Blue

Secondary Colors

- ⬤ Orange
- ⬤ Green
- ⬤ Purple

5

Orange on Land

Gila monsters are **venomous**.

Their bright orange color

warns others of danger.

Orange baboon tarantulas

are beautiful in color.

People keep them as pets.

Owners must be careful.

Their bites are very painful.

9

Orangutans are smart.

They use tools. Some tools
help them catch insects.

Orange in Air

Male Julia butterflies are bright.
Females have more black
markings than males.

13

Altamira orioles are orange.

They build long nests.

Nests can be 26 inches

(66 cm) long.

15

Ruddy shelducks are important in Tibet. Their orange color is the same as a **monk**'s robe.

Orange in Water

Most starfish are orange or brown. They have a great sense of smell.

19

Koi fish are raised to
be colorful. Orange is
a common color. This
practice started in Japan.

More Facts

- The name "orange" comes from the fruit.

- The color orange was named "yellow-red" before the 15th century.

- Orange is the color of fire, activity, danger, and autumn.

Glossary

monk – a member of a religious community. As a part of their beliefs, monks usually live a simple life. They do not own objects or have money.

primary color – a color that cannot be made by the mixing of other colors.

secondary color – a color resulting from the mixing of two primary colors.

venomous – putting venom into another animal by biting or stinging. Venom causes sickness or death.

Index

Altamira orioles 14

Gila monster 6

Japan 20

Julia butterfly 12

koi fish 20

nest 14

orange baboon tarantula 8

orangutan 10

ruddy shelducks 16

secondary color 4

starfish 18

Tibet 16

abdokids.com

Use this code to log on to abdokids.com and access crafts, games, videos, and more!

Abdo Kids Code:
AOK6962